NANTUCKET

a destination,
a community

Ene T. Bonnyay

Drumgarth LLC
Moraga, California

Library of Congress Control Number: 2002094553

ISBN: 0-9655360-2-5

Text & Photographs by Ene. T. Bonnyay
Text edited by Enid A. Goldberg
Designed by Ene & Laszlo Bonnyay

Printed by Kossuth Printing House
Budapest, Hungary

Published by Drumgarth LLC
Moraga, California

For Deborah and David, who love this island

We thank the following island friends and acquaintances who generously gave of their time to be photographed and permission to use the photos in this book: Dennis Metcalfe, Vallorie Oliver, Frank Day, Kenneth Aguiar, Alida Linda Lindstrom Storer, Pamela J. Bruce, The Rev. Dr. Warren Gritzke, Charles Rogerson, Ann and Charles Balas, Andrea Marks, Pauline L. Klek, DVM, Maria Waine, Noelle Walters, Eric Bogdahn, Gerry Scheide, Russell Mansfield.

From about May through Labor Day sixty thousand "seasonal" residents, vacationers, tourists – and now, with fast–ferry service, day-trippers – head for the six-by fourteen mile speck of sand off Cape Cod in the Atlantic Ocean called Nantucket. For these people, the "faraway land" is a destination that offers a temporary escape from their hectic pace in "America," a refuge in the healing powers of Nantucket's natural beauty; the calming effect of communion with sand, water, and sky; and also a dream and memory to take back off-island to other shores until perhaps the following year.

But Nantucket is also a community of approximately ten thousand natives, or locals, who are the backbone and the trustees of this magical place, which is definitely not a museum or theme park for visitors. They govern the island, provide all the year-round and seasonal services, and protect the integrity of this small and quaint oasis (no traffic lights, no neon signs, no fast food). They have the responsibility of keeping the island economically healthy and historically, architecturally, and aesthetically honest; and protecting its natural resources and controlling growth. The Land Bank, Nantucket Conservation Foundation, and Historic District Commission are among those entities that share in various aspects of these responsibilities.

Sankaty Head

Much of Nantucket's siren song and charm lies in the fact that almost half the island is forever protected from development, so one can still find a place of total solitude — not always marked on the map — to feel nature's rhythms and enjoy the gentle company of deer, pheasants, wild hares, beach birds, and seals.

From the time of its discovery and settlement, Nantucket really has had only a few options to sustain its economy. In the seventeenth and eighteenth centuries it was farming coupled with animal (sheep) husbandry. By the second half of the eighteenth century whaling for whale oil was becoming the island's most important industry, and by the first half of the nineteenth century whaling had become Nantucket's sole economic strength. The tiny island became known the world over as a major whaling capital. Sea captains built their incredible mansions in "Town" — still some of the man-made wonders of the island today.

Then followed a series of disastrous events in the mid-1800's — the fire of 1846 that destroyed much of the Town of Nantucket, the Gold Rush of 1849 that further depleted the population of the island with its lure of "instant wealth," and the blocking of the harbor by a major sand bar in 1850. Worst of all for the island's economy however, was the discovery of petroleum and its subsequent refining into kerosene. This was the death knell for the whaling industry and to the financial and social boon it had been for this island.

Not until the beginning of the 1900's did Nantucket begin to recover slowly as a result of the tourism industry. At first, some wealthy families began to frequent the Town and Siasconset ('Sconset) for "the season," but not until almost mid-century did the island really harvest a tourism crop that has sustained and enhanced its economy to this day. The same trend has, of course, also endangered some aspects of the island's character with large "trophy" homes, too many cars, and other threats to beaches and wildlife habitats.

Like most photography books, <u>Nantucket – a destination, a community</u> is a visual message about the island, not a verbal one. More detailed histories abound. A book of this scope can depict only a select few — a mere sampling — of the professionals, tradesmen, merchants, and artists who are representative of those who are essential to the life, unique character, continuity, as well as daily functioning of the place.

The year-round community of trustees lives with the island's year-round moods, the spring's welcome but unpredictable appearance with either daffodils, or snow, or both; with the glorious colors, skies, and waters of summer. Then there is the stark beauty of fall and winter, of desolate moors, gray skies reflected in gray waters, and spectacular storms. This off-season encourages the islanders to follow creative and artistic pursuits. For its size, Nantucket has an unusual number of painters, writers, photographers, and other artists, along with an equally sizable colony of craftsmen in various media. Little, cozy studios dot the island in the most unexpected places. Nantucket is a real island home and warm community that beckons to its shores many guests for a temporary but uniquely therapeutic and beautiful destination.

Madaket Road

Daffodils – the first harbingers of island spring

Daffodil Festival on Main Street

Daffodil Festival

Sleeping boats – Washington Street

Getting ready for the season off-shore

Nantucket Moorings' Dennis

Brant Point

Harbor view to Monomoy

The Steamship Authority

An island link

WELCOME TO
NANTUCKET

Town

Widow's walks

Architectural details have always been important

Architect Val

A never-ending

battle against

island weather

Frank

Kenny

Time out

Daily Breads

No fast foods

Moor's End Farm

Spring and summer gardening skills

'Sconset

GROW
DAMMIT!

Polpis Woods

Hidden retreats

A favorite destination for visitors

The Old Mill

Dionis

First Congregational Church

The island has many churches — the spiritual life of the community

Pam and Alida welcoming visitors

Tours with Rev. Dr. W. Gritzke

Life Saving Museum

Dionis

Dionis bikepath

Charles – basket maker in town

Bartlett Farm's truck on Main Street

Surfside

Beaches, the island's main attraction, are never far away

'Sconset

Wauwinet

Innkeeper Charles

Hotels, inns, bed and breakfasts and restaurants welcome seasonal visitors

Small gardens everywhere

Restaurant in 'Sconset

Trellises in town

Cisco

More beaches...

Cisco

Cisco

Madaket

Cliffside

CLIFFSIDE
BEACH

Madaket

Madaket sunsets

Bartlett's Ocean View Farm – since 1822

Andrea at Bartlett's

Dr. Klek at MSPCA

Pets — loyal companions are everywhere

Town

Cranberry bogs and harvest

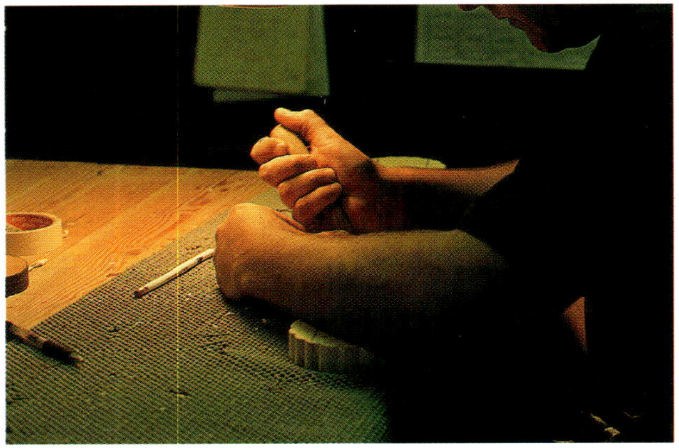

Quarterboards and other gilded signs are in

- neon is out

JIM'S
HAIR
CUTTING

THE COMPLETE KITCHEN

1845
HOUSE

CENTRE STREET INN
NANTUCKET

REAL
HEARD REAL ESTATE

Opening day for family scalloping

Checking the rings

Dinghy Dock

Town Pier

Nantucket's waters: Livelihood and sport

Great Point

LOBSTERS

BRANT POINT
MARINE

NANTUCKET ANGLERS CLUB
Sea Tel

Fall moor

Down time – the off-season

Storm clouds in Dionis

Dionis

Toward the 40th pole

Madaket

Washington Street

Sanford Farm – Nantucket Conservation Foundation

Waqutaquaib "kettlehole pond"

Pending storm

Mustard – Dionis

Gerri's cozy studio

South Wharf galleries

Artistic endeavors and the peace and quiet of off-season Town

Former Macy's warehouse and galleries

Brant Point

Russ in his basket workshop

The Atheneum – public library

Town – Main Street

NATIONAL

Main Street

ONGDONS' PHARMACY
ALLAN BELL R.PH
KENNETH KNUTTI R.PH
OPEN DAILY 8 to Late
ONGDONS
PHARMACY
NANTUCKET
PHARM

Almost Winter

Two pharmacies – a tradition in coexistence

Photo by Ann Balas

Photo by Ann Balas

Easy Street Basin

Perhaps an early spring